THE

INTROVERT'S

GUIDE

TO BECOMING A

MASTER NETWORKER

Jevonya Jenkins Allen

THE INTROVERT'S GUIDE TO BECOMING A
MASTER NETWORKER

Copyright © 2021

Published by Jevonya Allen

ISBN: 9798677014505

Printed in the United States of America

To reach the author, visit:

www.Jevonya.com

www.TwistedNetworking.com

"Networking is the #1 key to success in this game called life."

~ *Jevonya*

This book belongs to:

_____

NOTABLE INTROVERTS

Rosa Parks: Civil rights activist

Mark Zuckerberg: Co-founder and C.E.O. of Facebook

Bill Gates: Software developer, investor, and co-founder of Microsoft

Barak Obama: First African American President of the United States of America

Hilary Clinton: Lawyer, politician, presidential candidate and former First Lady of the United States of America

Warren Buffett: Investor, business tycoon, and philanthropist

Michael Jordan: Businessman and former professional basketball player

Albert Einstein: Physicist who developed the theory of relativity

CONTENTS

CONTENTS

INTRODUCTION

What comes to mind when you hear the word introvert? What feelings does this word conjure up in you? Do the words shy, sensitive, or unassertive come to mind? How about feelings of being misunderstood, overlooked, or unimportant? Now take a minute and think about the word networking. Do the words salesy, manipulative or inauthentic come to mind? How about feelings of being an imposter, uncomfortable or intimidated? What if I told you that all these words and feelings are real but by the end of this book, you will start to describe introverts as friendly, genuine and thoughtful. You will experience feelings of confidence, excitement and contentment. Networking will be enjoyable, fun and easy for you. Would you believe me? Well, that is exactly my goal for this book.

In writing this book, I desire for you to move beyond seeing introverts and networking in the negative light that is common today. I desire for you to own being an introvert and to capitalize on your disposition so that you can become the master networker that you want to be. If you identify with being an extrovert or an ambivert, I appreciate you taking time to see life and networking through the eyes of an introvert. Despite which disposition you identify with; my tips and insights will help you become a master networker.

You might be thinking to yourself; I don't really need to be a master networker; I just need to figure this thing out enough to grow my business. This thought is fair, but as you read on, you will begin to realize how mastering this art will not only grow your business but also enhance your quality of life and the lives of those around you.

As I prepare to share my tips with you, I cannot seem to shake the urge to go back in time to share a few of my life's defining moments that have shaped who I am today. I have titled these sections Head Start, my first job, and my first business.

Head Start

Growing up, I always felt different, but I was not quite sure why. My oldest memory of feeling different was when I was three years old, and I began attending the Head Start program. If you are not familiar with this social program, according to their website, "Head Start was designed to help break the cycle of poverty, providing preschool children of low-income families with a comprehensive program to meet their emotional, social, health, nutritional and psychological needs." (US Department of Health & Human Services)

While in Head Start, I had my first experience of bullying. There was this boy who would always pick on me. He would call me names and take my toys from me. I believe he even stole the crystal heart necklace that my mother let me wear on picture day.

On one occasion during nap time, as I was sleeping, he decided to flip over my cot, and I hit my face on the floor. I recall being in pain, being confused, and feeling embarrassed. I was too young to grasp why he treated me this way, but I recognized that there was something different about me because he did not do these things to anyone else.

I can remember occasionally playing with just one or two children but for the most part, I was perfectly content entertaining myself. When the teacher would ask questions, I knew the answers, but I would not speak up. I would much rather listen and observe than participate and have all eyes on me.

My First Job

When I was twelve years old, I was thrilled to get my first summer job working at the South Providence Boys and Girls Club. I was tasked with babysitting elementary school aged children. Occasionally, along with the more senior staff, we would take the children on field trips around the community. I vividly remember one of our outings when we took the children swimming at Brown University's pool. At that time, I could not swim but as I watched these children swimming and jumping off the diving boards, this voice in my head started saying *you should jump too*. This is my earliest recollection of hearing this voice within me that dared me to do something outside of my comfort zone.

In order to appease that voice that seemed to be getting louder and louder, I somehow conjured up a plan in my head so that I could jump. My plan consisted of having two other counselors—my network—wait in the pool for me just in case I did not come back up. I picked two counselors, and I nervously explained to them that I wanted to jump but could not swim; I needed them to wait in the middle of the pool for me just in case I started to drown. I was praying that they would talk me out of this crazy idea but to my dismay, they were willing to support me.

The pool was eighteen feet deep. The diving board options were either eight or twelve feet high. Now that I had my support system, my network, in place, I had to decide which ladder to jump from. That voice started up again and this time it was saying *twelve feet, twelve feet, twelve feet*. As I walked past the line of kids waiting to jump off the eight-foot ladder that voices said *you got this Jevonya, just jump*. Many years later, I would later come to realize what this voice was and how to harness its power.

I can clearly see myself holding onto the railings looking straight up to what seemed like an unending staircase. I try to lift my right leg and it feels like a ten-pound bag of lead. I do not quite know what comes over me but suddenly, I am climbing the ladder, knees shaking, heart pounding with probably the look of terror in my eyes. Now that once positive and encouraging voice quickly changed to a voice of fear and apprehension saying what are you thinking Jevonya, get off this ladder, you cannot even swim.

I eventually reached the top and walked out onto the diving board. I looked around and I felt like all eyes were on me which intensified my feelings of nervousness. But there was something intriguing, although scary, about viewing the room from that vantage point. I looked down and there were the other two counselors, my support system, my network, looking up at me as if to say *we got you Jevonya, just jump* and so I did.

As I hit the water and sank straight to the bottom, panic set in. I began flailing my arms and kicking my legs, screaming in my head for help, eyes wide open, bubbles everywhere, scared to death. But before I knew it, I was back at the surface and there was my support system, my network, ready and waiting to escort me out of the pool. I am proud to say that after that experience, I finally learned how to swim.

My First Business

Fall 2008, I had just taken in two more foster children, started dating my soon-to-be husband and then got married during a major snowstorm that December. Shortly after our wedding, our officiant, who was also a family friend and an insurance agent asked to meet with us about life insurance policies. Since we respected and trusted him, we gladly bought policies. A few months later, he reached out to me about two additional services that he started offering to his insurance clients but this time, he did not want to have a meeting, he just wanted me to watch a video.

I watched the video and what I saw was remarkably interesting. I immediately saw the value in the services that the company offered so I wanted to become a member. I was also intrigued by the business model and the vision that the company painted but I was content with my current lifestyle and I really could not see myself being a business owner. However, my friend was participating in a competition and I wanted to help him achieve his goals, so not only did I purchase the services, I also invested in the business opportunity.

If you are not familiar with the network marketing industry, you may have heard it also referred to as multi-level marketing, MLM, or direct sales. Network marketing is a strategy that companies use to sell a product or service by means of relationship referrals and word-of-mouth references. The company's sales force typically consumes the products or uses the services and they are also compensated through commissions and overrides for enlisting their personal contacts to become customers or business partners.

Although initially I was not considering working the business, once I signed on the dotted line, I was quickly swept into the recruiting system. Since my sponsor was participating in a competition, he needed me to have an in-home presentation to spread the word about my new business and the company. I was extremely uncomfortable, but I wanted to help him out, so I began to prepare for the launch of my first business.

I was in a unique situation because one of the women that I saw in that video—one of the company's top income earners—was going to be in town from California and she would be the one to facilitate my business launch. I clearly remembered her from the video, and I was beside myself knowing that such a successful woman was coming to my little humble home in South Providence.

I invited about twenty of my closest friends and family members, and five showed up. I was instructed to simply introduce our guest speaker and just watch and listen. As she stood in my living room, her petite frame and soft voice, I was captivated because she did not resemble the illusive depiction of success that had been seared into my subconscious since childhood.

She began to share her story, which initially did not resonate with me because she had a great start in life making a good income selling health club memberships. But then she mentioned that she was $40,000 in credit card debt when she met her sponsor who was retired at age 30 and living the lifestyle she always wanted. She shared with us that she discovered that the only way she was going to get out of debt and get wealthy was to start her own business and this network marketing company was the easiest business model that she could follow and the best compensation plan that she had ever seen.

She started part time, working her business one hour a day on her lunch break. Eight months later, she replaced her full-time income and officially retired from the work force at 25 years old. Because of her business, she was able to start contributing to a project to help families in undeveloped companies start their own businesses. She was also able to travel to Uganda, Africa on a mission trip to provide shoes for orphans. She has been able to be a full-time stay-at-home mom, using her passive income from building a team and residuals from memberships that renew each year to support her lifestyle.

After spending time with her and hearing her story, I was enthralled with the company. My thought was that if she could already be this financially successful in life and we were just a few months apart in age, then I could also use this vehicle to help me solve my financial woes.

I began regularly attending the company's business opportunity meetings and conferences throughout the United States. One of the most memorable conferences took place at the home office in Oklahoma. I rented a minivan and made the arduous thirty-two-hour drive along with four other brave souls.

Day one of the convention was just intoxicating. People from all walks of life, smiling, laughing, hugging, shaking hands and reveling in the positivity that consumed the air. The lights, the lanyards, the shiny pins, the atmosphere was simply electric. I felt like this was the group of business-minded people for me.

I was so impressed by the financial success stories that I could even see myself being a top income earner in the company. But I knew that I had work to do, and I was willing to do what was required of me. I started reading books, watching videos and listening to recordings on entrepreneurship, leadership and personal development. Much of my daily activities started to revolve around becoming a person who could be a financial success story too.

During my learning and growth process, I was introduced to various personality tests such as the Myers-Briggs Type Indicator®, The Paul Hertz Group PRINT survey and the TypeFinder® Personality Assessment. I was fascinated when I learned about introversion vs. extroversion. Every assessment that I had taken, I scored high for introversion so I started exploring what this meant for me and how this label would affect my existence. I was astonished to learn that in a 2019 Myers-Briggs study, 56.8% of people around the world reported that they prefer introversion. I was also quite amused to find out that January 2nd is World Introvert Day. Yes, we have a day dedicated to us.

Head Start opened my eyes to being different, my first job taught me the benefits of having a good support system, and my first business was the impetus for helping me to identify with being an introvert.

Typically, extroverts are expected to excel at networking while we struggle. Even though networking can be difficult, I have learned some techniques that have made it easier for me to honor being an introvert while also building an amazing network. In choosing to read this guide, you are showing that you understand and appreciate the value of networking and you desire to master this art in your life.

This guide is not going to be just filled with tips and stories. I am also going to challenge you to act on what you are learning. Some of the techniques might seem so basic that you may want to dismiss them, but I ask that you still act. You may even find that you are already employing some of the same techniques. If that is the case, see this guide as confirmation that you are on the right track. Also, share what you are learning to help other introverts embrace the notion that they too can become a master networker.

Throughout this guide, you will come across this symbol,

which represents a little extra insight that I thought would be helpful to you on your journey to becoming a master networker. This journey of building your network will require time, patience, endurance and hard work. One great thing about us introverts is that we are not afraid of hard work.

I am honored to be able to share my tips and insights with you. Read, internalize, act, and enjoy your well-deserved success!

Chapter 1: Personal Development

"The best investment you can make is in yourself."
(Warren Buffett)

While doing research, I stumbled across an article titled "How You Can Tell That You're an Introvert" (Cherry). The article listed 8 common signs:

1. Being around lots of people drains your energy.
2. You enjoy solitude.
3. You have a small group of close friends.
4. People often describe you as quiet and may find it difficult to get to know you.
5. Too much stimulation leaves you feeling distracted and unfocused.
6. You are very self-aware.
7. You like to learn by watching.
8. You are drawn to jobs that involve independence.

As I read through this short list, I could better understand why I felt and acted the way I did. I could also understand why other people would misjudge and mislabel me. On several occasions, I was called stuck up, I was told that I thought I was better than everyone else, I was told that I did not belong and that I did not fit in. People would even ask me why I was so quiet. I did not know how to respond but over the years these comments had me questioning my own existence. You may have had a similar experience, and what tends to happen is that when you are consistently misjudged and mislabeled, you can start to have internal conflicts, negative self-talk, destructive behaviors, and low self-esteem. I felt uncomfortable, unimportant, and unseen. I became even more introspective, struggled with weight issues and just coasted aimlessly through my life. All the while, I was walking around with a smile on my face as if everything were fine. I felt like people wanted to change me, so eventually I wanted to change me but there were certain things that I could not because this was my nature, my disposition, the way I was born.

Another article that I read said that introverts:

- Think before speaking and acting.
- Listen more than they speak.
- Excel in situations requiring complex thought and preparation.
- Avoid being the center of attention.

This description also fit me perfectly and it brought me so much comfort and relief to know that nothing was wrong with me and that there were other people out there who were just like me.

One online dictionary describes personal development as activities that improve awareness and identity, enhances the quality of life, and contributes to the realization of dreams and aspirations. I appreciate this description because I believe building a business and a network should enhance the quality of our lives as well as contribute to the realization of our dreams and aspirations. As the description starts off, we must first improve our awareness and identity. But why do we need to improve our awareness and identity? One primary reason is because we need to attract a network of people who can help us. I use the word "attract" because our goal is to draw people who will willingly share their knowledge, expertise and experiences with us. This might sound completely self-serving, but I want to impress upon you that these relationships will be mutually beneficial because we are all both teachers and students. You have many years of knowledge and life experiences that you will also share with them. You both will bring something different to the proverbial table which will help both of you to grow. I have witnessed this beautiful symbiotic relationship emerge between myself and my network. The better I become, the more I am able to add value to my network which in turn adds value to me. This dynamic richly enhances the lives of everyone involved.

As introverts, we tend to keep most things to ourselves. But personal development will help you share your story, your thoughts and your feelings which is a key factor in becoming a master networker. People need and want to hear your voice.

Becoming a master networker is all about getting people who know, like, and trust you enough to share information and resources with you. These individuals will also be more likely to do business with you, and they will feel comfortable referring you to their family, friends, associates, and colleagues. In order to build these relationships, you must be comfortable in your skin, and you must know, like, and trust yourself first.

When I started my first business, I was mentally, emotionally, physically, and financially in a bad place. I had three young children, a house that I could not afford, and a bad marriage. I was overweight and had over $100,000 in student loan debt. I felt socially awkward, and my self-esteem was shot. All I could see were these areas where I felt like I was failing in life.

Not only was I dissatisfied with my life but my natural inclination as an introvert is to avoid the limelight. I would rather not express my thoughts. I would prefer to listen to others rather than have others listen to me. When I would meet someone, my nerves would get the best of me. I would do everything to deflect questions so that the attention was not on me. I recall being at a business opportunity meeting and everyone was talking, laughing, and enjoying the association whereas I was in the back, snacking, trying to avoid all eye contact and conversations. But I knew that for me to achieve the levels of success that I desired; I would have to do something differently.

Personal development was exactly what I needed. Personal development helped me to take an in-depth look at myself and understand who I was; it helped me to embrace my strengths and find ways to compensate for my weaknesses. I found ways to reject my defeatist mindset and see beyond my negative situation in my life.

Because I was doing personal development and started gradually surrounding myself with people who thought differently than I did, I was able to successfully climb out of that hole just like my support system was able to help me climb out of that pool. One person who became a huge part of my network happened to be someone who found my business card and called while I was walking through a home improvement store. He was in a different network marketing company, so he was reaching out to network with me, but I was unfamiliar with networking. Although we were from entirely different walks of life, we just connected on a deeper level. I became his client, and he became my client. He invited me to networking events, and I invited him to my religious meeting. He would talk to me about his upbringing, and I would share with him how I was raised. He would talk to me about finances, and I would just absorb everything he was teaching me. Meeting him led me to attending more networking events, which helped me to meet more people who embodied success principles. I eventually joined a business networking organization with him and in time, I became part of their leadership team.

Since we are typically introspective, personal development sounds like it should be easy for us, but I found that it's probably the hardest of all the techniques in this guide. I believe that personal development is challenging for introverts because we enjoy the bubble that we have created for ourselves and personal development pushes us outside of our comfort zone. We tend to be content with avoiding risks, but I'm here to tell you that scaling that business, launching that nonprofit organization, writing that book, and living that lifestyle that you envision can't be accomplished by allowing your fears and insecurities to stifle your actions.

How to use Personal Development to become a Master Networker

1. Schedule time to read, watch videos, and listen to educational recordings that contain information designed to help you to become a better version of yourself.

2. Have a notebook, a pen and some highlighters readily available.

3. Set a timer to keep yourself committed to your schedule and goal.

4. Underline, highlight and take notes on what resonates with you and aligns with your values and aspirations so that you can look back on the important things later.

5. Ask other people for their recommended reading and networking tips.

6. Share what you have learned with others.

 You might enjoy some of the content from Valuetainment, Alux, Audible and Team Fearless Motivation.

TAKE ACTION

✓ This week determine how much time your schedule will permit you to spend engaging in personal development each day. If you already have a regular reading or listening schedule, consider increasing the amount of time by 5 minutes.

✓ Pick one book from the suggested reading list found in Appendix A, select a book from your bookshelf or order a book that you have been longing to read.

✓ Conduct an online search for videos, podcasts and audiobooks on personal development. Watch, listen and take notes.

Chapter 2: Affirmations

"It's the repetition of affirmations that lead to belief. Once that belief becomes a deep conviction, things begin to happen." (Muhammad Ali)

When I was first introduced to affirmations, I was in a desperate place, mentally, emotionally, and financially. Between my childhood traumas dating back to that experience in Head Start and the current situations that I found myself in, my self-esteem was shot, and my self-talk was excessively negative. I had also unconsciously internalized those negative perceptions about introverts that are so prevalent in our society. Those misconceptions that we are shy, hard to get to know, self-absorbed and aloof. Can you relate? By unknowingly adopting those beliefs, our self-talk tends to be negative, which will hinder how we show up in the world.

Simply put, affirmations are small statements that are positive and can reinforce a thought or idea, which helps defeat negative self-talk and can bolster confidence.

As I mentioned in the prior chapter, becoming a master networker requires us to attract people. To attract people, we must first be attractive. I do not mean in the sense of physical appearance. Being attractive is about how you carry yourself, how you feel and think about yourself, what you say and how you say it, and how you make other people feel. Being attractive requires that you have a positive self-image. It is not about having an ego but knowing your value and worth and sharing it with the people you meet. Having a positive self-image, owning your introversion, and sharing your gifts will draw people closer to you. People will not only want to be in your presence, but they will want other people to connect with you as well.

When my coach first suggested the idea of me writing a book, my initial reaction was total rejection. The idea of being an author just did not fit into the thoughts that I had about who I was. I could not see myself as an author. I did not like the idea of writing a book because I knew the process would be daunting and that once published, I would be opening myself up to more of the world's judgments and perceptions. I shared my apprehension with him, and our conversation reminded me how I had used affirmations in the past to get over challenging situations. During one session, I came up with the affirmation: "I am a self-published author." Throughout this year-long process of writing, editing and publishing this book, I would recite my new affirmation. I wrote it down, I recorded myself saying it and I would listen to it repeatedly. Eventually, I became comfortable with the idea of being an author so much so that I found myself proudly and openly telling people that I had authored a book. The fact that you are now reading this guide is proof that affirmations can work because what started off as a huge source of anxiety subsequently became a source of joy.

Affirmations help you to see yourself in the future. They help you to change negative thoughts, which we all have, into positive ones. Affirmations help you to concentrate and act on your goals. Ultimately, what you think about yourself impacts how you feel, which determines how you interact with the world.

How to use Affirmations to become a

Master Networker

To create meaningful affirmations, begin with an analysis of your life and goals. On page 42, you will find a visual aid that I use with my business consulting clients called "My Circle of Life." This activity guides me in assessing the eight main areas of my life:

1. Health
2. Environment
3. Growth
4. Recreation
5. Romance
6. Community
7. Career
8. Income

This visual aid will help you to better understand which areas you are flourishing in and which areas need some improvements.

Assign a rating from 1 to 10 for each of these areas. A score of 1 indicates that you are unsatisfied in this area and a score of 10 indicates that this part of your life is amazing. Do not over-think the process. Often the first number that pops into your head is the most appropriate.

MY CIRCLE OF LIFE

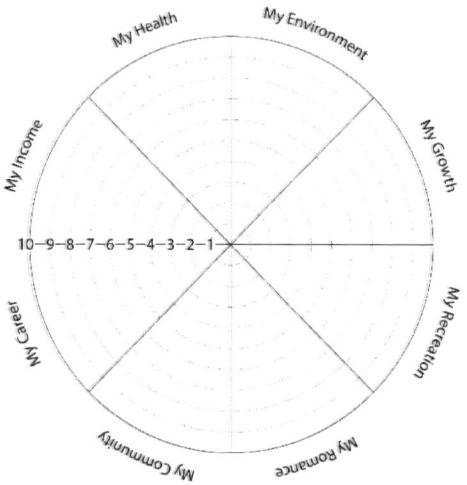

Rate yourself on your level of satisfaction in each major area of your life. Plot each score on the chart and connect the dots. The objective is to get as close to a well-rounded circle as possible. We will always have something to work on and that is O.K.

<u>MY CIRCLE OF LIFE GRADING KEY</u>

My Health = my diet, sleep, exercise, spirituality, relaxation, mental and emotional health

My Environment = my home and physical environment

My Growth = my personal development plan, educational regime, and learning opportunities

My Recreation = my hobbies, exploration, travel and fun

My Romance = my significant other or prospective partner

My Community = my relationship with friends, family and the wider community

My Career = the work that I do or want to do to add value and to feel fulfilled

My Income = my current streams of income and the money I have available to support my lifestyle

Once you identify the areas where you feel the least satisfied, you can create affirmations for improvements. Here is how to incorporate affirmations effectively in your life:

1. Write your affirmation down in your journal, on an index card, print them on a piece of paper or type them in the notes section of your cell phone.
2. Place your affirmations in highly visible, easily accessible places in your home, office and car.
3. Read your affirmation as often as possible, especially when you are having negative moments.
4. Record yourself saying your affirmations and listen to them frequently.
5. Share your affirmations with trusted friends and family members.

Here are a few sample affirmations that I have benefited from:

- I am proud to be an introvert.
- The world needs my ideas, passion and heart.
- I am a master networker.
- I easily attract my ideal clients.
- Taking time for myself is o.k.
- I am a person who has a lot to offer others.
- I am getting better at networking every day.
- I am excited to build and grow my network.

There is a powerful video on **Team Fearless Motivation's** YouTube channel entitled "I AM." The video starts off by saying that "I AM" are the two most powerful words in the English language. It goes on to say that whatever you say after "I AM" will shape your life. So, when creating an affirmation, do your best to start it with the words "I AM" because as the video suggests, what you speak after "I AM" and what you believe after saying the words "I AM" will control your decisions and shape your life. Make sure you go check out this inspiring video.

TAKE ACTION

✓ Complete the circle of life exercise. It's ok to write in this book. This is your study guide.

✓ Create one affirmation for each area of your life where you rated your level of satisfaction a 7 or below.

✓ Write down your affirmations.

✓ Post your affirmations in convenient places around your home, office and in your vehicle.

✓ Use your phone to record yourself saying your affirmations.

✓ Read and listen to affirmation every day for at least one week.

Chapter 3: Powerful Marketing Script

"If you can't explain it simply, you don't understand it well enough."

(Albert Einstein)

You might be saying to yourself; I have never heard of a powerful marketing script; this sounds kind of complicated. Let me alleviate any anxiety right now by saying you *have* heard of a powerful marketing script—you just may have heard it called a sixty second commercial or an elevator pitch. Whoever coined the terms sixty second commercial and elevator pitch were in the right frame of mind when focusing on the length, but I don't feel that these terms give enough credence to the importance of this statement.

Have you ever asked someone what they do, and after listening to all their jargon and bantering for what seems forever, you still have no clue? I am sure you have been in this situation a time or two. The best way not to be this person is to create a powerful marketing script.

Your powerful marketing script will be a quick synopsis of your background, expertise, credentials, experiences and/or business. It can also be a short description of your idea, products or company. The script will explain the value you bring in such a way that any listener can understand it in a short period of time. Done right, it will help you introduce yourself to new connections in a concise and compelling way. Your powerful marketing script will ignite interest and make you memorable.

When I started on my entrepreneurial journey, I worked with my mother at her home daycare. I had recently joined the network marketing company that I mentioned in the introduction. Going from working with little children to needing to learn sales was totally out of my comfort zone.

For some reason, the company that I worked for did not want us to use the company's name when talking to people. We were trained to tell stories and share the features of the services. There were so many conflicting training philosophies that I sought out training from other avenues. I felt like I was being taught how to sell the services but never how to market so when I stepped onto the networking scene, I felt like a deer in headlights, totally unprepared. But I quickly figured out that I need to come up with something to say if I didn't want to look like an amateur in the business arena.

Since we do not like to be the center of attention, the thought of sharing our scripts with others can be a source of discomfort. If you have this apprehension, refer to Chapter 2 and create an affirmation to reduce this feeling a bit. Taking time to prepare and rehearsing your script will ease the nervousness and the tendency to stumble over your words.

Your powerful marketing script is also essential because it will help your network know what kind of work you do and how to introduce you to prospective clients, referral sources and investors. If people do not understand what you do, then they will not be able to use your services or refer you to other people. For you to transfer this information to others, you first need to thoroughly understand the kind of work that you do and be clear on the value that you bring to the marketplace. It will also come in handy at networking events, which we will discuss a little later in Chapter 5.

 Make your powerful marketing script so simple that even a 5th grader can understand who you are and what you do. Keep it short and sweet, focus on the essentials, be positive and persuasive and most of all practice, practice, practice.

How to Use Your Powerful Marketing Script to Become a Master Networker

The goal is to create your script in such a way that you can memorize it and reproduce it. Your powerful marketing script should be simple and clear, so much so that other people should just "get it." This is valuable when using social media because your connections will ask you what you do, and you can easily copy and paste your script.

Your powerful marketing script will include a combination of the following elements:

1. Who you are
2. What you do
3. Why you do it
4. Who your ideal client is

Here is an example of one of my powerful marketing scripts:

"I am an author, a speaker and a networking coach. I enjoy working with people who understand the need to network but are finding networking to be challenging. I help my clients through my book, my online course and my company, Twisted Networking, where we facilitate in-person and virtual networking events.

TAKE ACTION

✓ Write out your powerful marketing script.

✓ Record and listen to yourself saying it.

✓ Whenever someone asks you what you do, use your script.

✓ Create opportunities to use your powerful marketing script by asking people what they do first.

✓ Email your powerful marketing script to me at **Jevonya@twistednetworking.com** and I will personally respond to offer you some support.

Chapter 4: Social Media

"Social media is the ultimate equalizer. It gives a voice and a platform to anyone willing to engage."

(Amy Jo Martin)

As I write this, according to Statista, the global #1 business research and data platform, there are "3.6 billion users on social networks worldwide. Up from 2.86 billion in 2017 with a projected 4.41 billion by 2025." (Statista)

You might cringe at using social media because of the bad reputation that it has for being a place for selfies, pictures of food, vacation, pets, hacking, and political battles. Some people misuse this tool and others have different motives for being on social media, but ultimately it was created to help people connect and communicate faster. Facebook founder Mark Zuckerberg says that "by giving people the power to share, we're making the world more transparent."

As introverts, the thought of transparency can be unnerving since we would rather not be the center of attention—we would prefer just to watch and observe others. I am here to tell you that there is absolutely nothing wrong with not wanting to be the center of attention. There is nothing wrong with being slow to reveal your emotions or opinions, and there is nothing wrong with watching and being observant.

That said, since our natural inclination is not to want to share or engage, by idly sitting back we can miss out on opportunities to encourage, support and help others which is a primary proponent of becoming a master networker. By just watching, or by not even having any social media accounts, we can miss out on those occasions when our "friends" or connections are telling us what is going on in their lives and how we can help them. By posting on social media, people are offering us valuable information about what they like, what they dislike, their hopes and their dreams, their anxieties and their needs. Social media can be our best marketing tool if we have the right mindset and use it to our advantage. Like author Erik Qualman says, we do not have a choice on whether we do social media. The question instead is: How well will we do it?

I remember when Facebook first started, it was initially for college students, and you needed a college email address to sign up. Everyone on my college campus was getting an account, so of course, I got one too. I just scrolled and observed for a long time before I decided to start posting. I began by posting a positive quote. Something that would uplift my friends. Then I would occasionally post pictures of my family, pose a question, or create an interactive post such as a word search. As with most things, the more you use them, the easier they become, and social media is no different. In time, I became a little more comfortable to where I started posting group pictures with me in them. Eventually, I became so comfortable that I can now proudly post selfies when I look and feel good about myself.

Social media has allowed me to connect with thousands of people and promote my business for free while expending little energy. Think of your social media platform(s) as free marketing tools. The more people who see your name and your posts, the bigger your network will become. But always keep in mind that social media is a limited platform. The most fulfilling relationships in your life will not be sustained purely over social media. You will eventually need to transition to in-person connections or use video conferencing software. Nothing beats seeing facial expressions and hearing voices in real time. But social media is a great way to meet and connect with people who you might not otherwise meet and if used properly, social media can be a comfortable, cost and time effective tool to help you build your network.

I add friends and new connections daily. I get quite a few connection requests so much so that at one time, I maxed out Facebook's capacity of 5,000 contacts. I set parameters as to who I add, but I am aware that I need to grow my network consistently because I once heard it said, "Your net worth is equal to your network." The more extensive your network, the more lives you can touch, which in turns gives you a real sense of community and you will also have a support system to fall back on.

Once I make a new connection, I immediately send them a "Thank you for connecting with me" message to their inbox. I do this because I genuinely want to make a new connection, not just have another person on my list. If I decide to send them something in the future, it's not an awkward situation because I have already initiated an exchange.

I now use post planning software for my business pages. I also regularly interact on my personal pages by commenting, liking, sharing other people's posts, and participating in groups. When my connections need my services or know someone that I can help, they are already familiar with who I am and what I do. For example, when I completed my business consulting certification, I posted a picture holding my certificate. By posting that picture, within days, I had my first consulting client.

I view social media as a way for me to get my information out there without feeling like I am bothering people. It makes marketing more comfortable for me as an introvert. By being consistent on my social media platforms, I have been able to build that *like, know, trust* factor that is vital to business success. I am still always observing so that I can reciprocate when I see that someone is in need or has something to offer.

How to use Social Media to become a

Master Networker

If you are not on social media, I recommend that you pick a platform and set up an account this week. If you are apprehensive, I understand. Many people are afraid of social media. Getting hacked is a real threat. People having a glimpse into your personal life can be scary and social media can be time-consuming *if you allow it to be*. But we need to see social media as part of our strategy to become master networkers. Remember that you will have control over your settings and who you interact with. I love the unfollow, block, snooze for 30 days, and unfriend features provided by some platforms. I currently use Facebook, Instagram, Twitter, LinkedIn, YouTube, Pinterest and Clubhouse. There are other platforms, and each has its own pros and cons so do your research and determine which is best for your personality, business and networking goals.

 Try not to worry about comments or likes; just do the activity. Keep in mind that just as you have been watching and not interacting, other people are doing the same thing. Also, be cautious of what you post and what you like because you can inadvertently polarize your audience.

If you are already active on social media but would like to increase your engagement and following this week, I challenge you to use this posting schedule:

Monday: Post something motivational. This can be a meme, a graphic, a quote, anything that is positive and inspirational and if you know how, make use of hashtags.

Tuesday: Go through your suggested people list and add 10 new people. Each platform calls this list by a different name. Essentially this is a list of people who the platform thinks you should connect with or follow. To protect myself and ensure the integrity of my network, here are the criteria that I use in growing my network on social media. Keep in mind there are always exceptions:

1. The prospective new contact should have a profile picture of their face.
2. We should have at least ten mutual connections.

3. After I scroll through their page, they must appear to be someone I would talk to in real life.

Wednesday: Give someone in your network a shout-out. This could be a friend, family member, colleague, or client. If possible, tag the person and just say thank you for being you.

Thursday: Go through your suggested people list again and follow the same steps you followed on Tuesday.

Friday: Comment something that you are excited about or use your search engine of choice to find interactive social media posts. Interactive social media posts typically have a graphic that encourages your friends to comment and engage with you. Once your friends comment on your post, be sure that you respond to their comments and engage back.

TAKE ACTION

✓ Have a professional headshot taken. Social media loves pictures.

✓ Create professional profiles on two or more social media platforms. If your pages are already set-up, review your profiles checking for consistency, relevancy and transparency.

✓ Adopt the suggested posting schedule as part of your marketing strategy.

✓ Spend thirty minutes to one hour on social media every day. Use this time to post content and to engage with others.

✓ If applicable, research post planning programs for your business pages.

✓ If you are really daring, go live or record and share a video once or twice a week.

Chapter 5: Networking Events

"Everyone should build their network before they need it."
(Dave Delaney)

Mastering networking events was by no means an easy feat for me, but because I knew I had something of value to share and I also needed to learn what was going on in the local business community, I was determined to confront my fears one event at a time.

Getting comfortable at networking events has been a slow process which to be completely honest, I still struggle with at times. But these events have taught me that I needed to be visible in the community. I had to get out of my comfort zone and connect with people.

As an introvert, large groups can be overwhelming. Socializing can be mentally and physically draining. Just the thought of talking about ourselves in front of people can cause us significant anxiety. Most people, even extroverts, report having a severe fear of public speaking.

I vividly remember the feeling that I had at my first in-person networking event. Walking into a room full of strangers sent me into my first and only panic attack. I had to leave the venue and go outside because I was hyperventilating, sweating profusely and shaking unlike anything I had ever experienced. After saying a quick, silent prayer, I was somehow able to regain my composure enough to go back inside. I went straight to the bathroom, and then I stood around the food stations just surveying the room. I was so afraid to move because in my head I had already made a fool of myself and I felt like all eyes were on me. So, I just watched everyone in their little cliques tucked away in various corners, laughing and having a grand old time all the while I felt so out of place, totally outside of my comfort zone. Eventually another newbie spoke to me and we provided each other a source of comfort.

Following that experience, I started getting invited to various networking events, each with slightly different formats. I attended events hosted by the **Chamber of Commerce,** which is made up of paying members located within or near the geographical area the chamber serves. I attended **Lead Groups** which consist of paying members who typically meet weekly. Each lead group follows the same meeting agenda and procedures. Lead groups only allow one person per industry to be a member. I attended events hosted by various **Associations** which are made up of paying members who come together based on some mutual interest such as women's groups, young professional groups and African American groups. I attended **Open Networking** events. That first event that I attended was an open networking event. At these events, people from all walks of life come together to make new connections. These events may be free or require a nominal fee for entry.

I would accept the invitations even though I would be a nervous wreck before, during, and afterward. While I was at the event, I would usually watch and observe. I would interact sporadically, primarily nodding my head and listening to others speak. Quite honestly, I had no clue what most of the people were talking about because they had not yet mastered their powerful marketing script. But I loved the thought process behind bringing like-minded businesspeople together to share, support, and pass referrals.

All my observations and uncomfortable moments eventually led me to creating a business networking organization, where we host in-person and virtual networking events that are designed to be interactive, fun, and are introvert friendly. Our events are a fusion of the positive aspects of each of those networking event formats that I had attended. Our primary objective is to help our attendees take their business, cause, organization, or career to the next level through meaningful relationships in a comfortable, welcoming, low pressure environment. I have also franchised my system for others to follow to host their own networking events.

All these events have impressed upon me that success in business depends on who you know and who knows you. Former First Lady of the United States of America, Michelle Obama says "success isn't about how much money you make; it's about the difference you make in people's lives." **New York Times bestselling author, public speaker, and former Yahoo! executive Tim Sanders has been noted for his quote, "Your network is your net worth."**

Developing relationships and making new connections opens doors to more opportunities which in turn will increase your value and the value of those around you.

Even though networking events can be stressful for us, understanding the benefits can help to allay our apprehension. Here are some reasons why we should attend networking events:

Build Your Confidence:

- Practice your Powerful Marketing Script
- Develop public speaking skills
- Motivate you to socialize and get outside of your comfort zone

Build Meaningful Relationships:

- Meet new like-minded people
- Add other professionals to your network

- Get people to know, like, and trust you

Advance Your Business:

- Generate referrals
- Economical marketing strategy
- Stay current with trends by learning from speakers outside of your industry
- Get fresh ideas and solutions for your business
- Find new business partners, employees and investors

Establish and Expand Your Sphere of Influence:

- Be a resource for other businesses
- Meet other influencers
- Help more people

How to use Networking Events to become a

Master Networker

First, if you are going to attend an in-person event, ask someone to go with you so that you do not have to go it alone. If you are daring or are in any way like me and just prefer to do most things alone, the tips in Chapter 1 on personal development coupled with affirmations from Chapter 2 will help you mentally prepare and will help you while at the event.

Second, since mingling expends a lot of energy for us, you must plan well and put these events on your calendar. I prefer afternoon events, and I schedule a nap or a break following them so that I can recharge my energy.

I love virtual networking events, but these too can be overwhelming for me if they are not done correctly. When Covid hit, I had to quickly convert our in-person networking events to virtual events ensuring that they still captured all the elements that make our events unique while also respecting being an introvert. I am proud to say that our events are still thriving and are still introvert friendly. Extroverts even rave about them.

Third, you will need to create networking goals. For example, for an in-person event, plan to stay at the venue for at least one hour and set the goal of getting and giving out two business cards. If you don't have any business cards and you plan on attending in-person events, set a goal to order some immediately. Vistaprint is a great source for professional and inexpensive business cards. For virtual events, plan to get the contact information for two people before the event concludes.

Here are a few things to consider before selecting an event to attend:

- Who is hosting the event?
- When and where is the event being held?
- Is there a cost, if so, how much?
- How many people will be in attendance?
- What industries will be represented?
- Will you have an opportunity to speak?
- Is there a structure to the event?
- Will you receive the attendee list in advance or afterwards?
- Is the group membership-based? If so, are you able and willing to make the time and financial commitment?

TAKE ACTION

✓ Set a goal to attend one to two networking events a month.

✓ Find a networking buddy for in-person events.

✓ Perform an internet search for networking events near you.

✓ Look for upcoming networking events on your social media platforms.

✓ Register for an in-person or a virtual Twisted Networking event.

 The more you attend, the more comfortable you will become, but the nervousness and apprehension might always be there. The book *Feel the Fear and Do It Anyway* by Dr. Susan Jeffers inspires us with dynamic techniques and profound concepts that have helped countless people grab hold of their fears and move forward with their lives. Inside you will discover the vital 10-step process that helps you outtalk the negative chatterbox in your brain.

Chapter 6: One-on-Ones

"Pretend that every single person you meet has a sign around his or her neck that says, 'Make me feel important.' Not only will you succeed in sales, but you will also succeed in life." (Mark Kay Ash)

Mary Kay Ash, businesswoman and founder of Mary Kay Cosmetics passed away on November 22, 2001. At the time of her death, Mary Kay's personal fortune was $98 million, and her company had more than $1.2 billion in sales and an international sales force of more than eight hundred thousand in at least three dozen countries. Mary Kay's success is evidence that she valued people and that throughout her life, she made time to connect with others on a more interpersonal level.

In the last chapter, we discussed networking events. These events are great ways to meet new people but once the event is over, those new relationships need to be cultivated. One-on-one meetings are the next step in building your network. These meetings will allow you to get to know other people on a deeper level. One-on-ones are a dedicated space on your calendar for an open-ended and anticipated conversation with your new contact. During this meeting, you will have the opportunity to learn more about your new contact. You will learn about who they are, gather more detailed information about their line of work, and determine whether potential exists to work together or to assist each other. You will also have a chance to share more about who you are, what you do and how you can help them.

These types of meetings are ideal for introverts because while we thrive in small groups, we excel in one-on-one situations. In her article The Importance of Networking (and How to Do It Well), Career Coach Amanda Augustine states "networking isn't merely the exchange of information with others, and it's certainly not about begging for favors. Networking is about establishing and nurturing long-term, mutually beneficial relationships with the people you meet." (Augustine) Participating in one-on-one meetings is a great way to turn cold leads into warm referral sources. When your new contact knows of something that could benefit you, you will be top of mind. Your new contact will talk well of you to others, which is vital in establishing your credibility and likability with other professionals. You will likewise be able to reciprocate these good deeds.

After I meet someone at a networking event and I feel that we had some synergy, I schedule a one-on-one meeting. For in-person meetings, we typically meet at one of our offices, a coffee shop, hotel lobby or a restaurant. I have even met up for a walk in the park. I try to make sure that the location is comfortable and convenient for both of us. Since I do not like talking too much about myself and I am very inquisitive, I usually let the other person do most of the talking while I ask questions and listen. I briefly talk about what I do, but I usually manage to turn the conversation back onto them. This allows me to learn so much about people while developing trust and a deeper bond. I have come to realize that many people are not listened to, not even by their family members. By listening to people, and as Mark Kay Ash mentioned, making people feel important, you can automatically draw them to you.

This process is quite like making friends. Networking and making friends both require listening, trust and mutual respect. If at this point, the word networking still has a negative connotation to you, think of networking as making new friends. Many of the people that I have met through networking have become some of my closest friends and confidants.

One-on-ones have allowed me to learn about industries that I do not have time to study. For example, one-on-ones with coaches, accountants, lawyers, realtors, financial planners, mortgage brokers and other sales reps will give you a glimpse into these professions. The knowledge and experience that these individuals bring to the meeting will enhance your knowledge base which in turn will make you more useful to everyone you meet because you can share valuable information or connect them to someone who can help them.

Today, I still have a few weekly slots on my calendar where I can have one-on-one meetings. I believe that we always have room for new friends and that you can never have enough people in your network.

How to use One-on-Ones to become a

Master Networker

Scheduling one-on-ones can seem like just another thing added to your "to-do" list. Finding time to meet with people when you already have a full schedule can be challenging. Spending time with our family, friends, work and current clients must be our top priorities, but making time to meet new people and to grow our network has to also rank high on the priority list. The key is to set a goal and to have a consistent time block on your schedule for one-on-ones.

To better manage my time, I use an electronic calendar that allows me to schedule various types of appointments. I block off 2 hours a week for one-on-one meetings. My goal is to meet one-on-one with at least one new person a week. I love virtual meetings because they allow me to meet with people all over the world and I can easily attend back-to-back meetings.

The objective of your one-on-one is to learn as much as you can about the other person. Skillfully asking questions will show that you are interested in others which will in turn help you to grow your network. Here are some great questions for your one-on-ones:

1. How did you get started in your field/business?
2. What do you like most about what you do?
3. What are some of your current challenges?
4. Who is your ideal client?
5. How would I know if someone would be a great connection for you?

 Once you start asking others these questions, the natural progression is for people to ask you in return. Take some time to answer these questions yourself so that when you are asked, you are prepared.

Another technique that can help you to gather information on one-on-ones and at networking events is to follow an acronym, F.O.R.M., which stands for Family, Occupation, Recreation, and Motivation. People typically love to talk about their family, their work, their hobbies, and their inspirations. Asking questions and talking about these areas of life is a sure way to win with people and to become a master networker.

TAKE ACTION

✓ Set the goal to have at least one one-on-one per week.

✓ Block off one-on-one time on your calendar.

✓ Within the next seven days, schedule a 30-minute meeting with someone you do not know well but who you would like to establish a professional relationship with. Pick a person from one of your social media accounts, a networking event, or a business card that you have lying around.

✓ To schedule the meeting, simply reach out and say or type:

"Hi (insert first name),

I'd like to learn more about what you are working on. Are you open to a conversation?"

✓ Throughout the conversation, use the F.O.R.M. technique and the sample questions.

✓ Listen and take notes.

Chapter 7: Following Up

"Diligent follow-ups and follow-through will set you apart from the crowd and communicates excellence."

(John Maxwell)

I am an avid John Maxwell reader. If you are not familiar with Mr. Maxwell, he is a leadership expert, speaker and author. He has written many books, primarily focusing on leadership. Titles include *The Maxwell Daily Reader-365 Days of Insight to Develop the Leader Within You and Influence Those Around You, Everyone Communicates Few Connect, and The 21 Irrefutable Laws of Leadership.* Mr. Maxwell speaks annually for Fortune 500 companies, international government leaders and a diverse array of other organizations.

I love Mr. Maxwell's quote because the word "excellence" is one of my core values. By "excellence," I mean making sure that I am always giving and doing my best. I have also learned that excellence is a common trait among introverts. Mr. Maxwell adds that our goal should be to set ourselves apart from the crowd. Most people never follow-up or follow-through on their commitments. This communicates a level of unprofessionalism and unreliability which will slowly breed distrust. In the business arena, credibility is everything. If you say you are going to do something, you must do it, or your reputation will be tarnished. I am sure you have heard that bad news travels faster than good news. If you value your reputation and want to make a good impression, following-up and following-through will help you accomplish this goal.

Since introverts typically are more comfortable with written communication, sending an email, a text message, or a handwritten note makes this an easy tip. Taking this extra step that most people ignore will help you become a master networker because people will remember you. They will remember how you made them feel. They will appreciate that you made this effort. You will be viewed as considerate and thoughtful. Although they might not respond, rest assured they received your message, and it made them view you in a positive light.

I recently had a situation where I wanted to purchase some jewelry from one of my Facebook friends. I reached out to her and told her what I wanted and that I was ready to buy, but she did not respond in what I deemed a timely manner. I decided to purchase from someone else at the same company. A week later, the original rep sent me a message, looking for the sale. I had to inform her that I had already purchased what I wanted from someone else. She lost an easy deal because she was not diligent in her follow-up or follow-through. Now when I want to purchase jewelry, the likelihood of me reaching out to her is slim to none nor am

I compelled to refer her to others in my network. The adage *fortune is in the immediate follow-up* always rings true.

How to use Following Up to become a

Master Networker

After meeting someone at an event or after a one-on-one, I send a follow-up message within 24 to 48 hours. Over the years, to follow-up, I have used emails, text messages, private messages, and handwritten notes. Emails, texts, and private messages are the easiest and most convenient tools, but the handwritten note is the most powerful.

I create standardized templates that I can quickly reproduce through all these modes of written communications. For example, after a one-on-one, I will send a follow-up note that says:

"Hi [insert first name],

Thank you for taking the time out of your schedule to meet with me. I appreciate you sharing a bit of your knowledge.

If I come across someone who I think would be a great connection for you, I will be sure to reach back out."

Respectfully yours,

Jevonya Allen M.A. Ed

Creator and Chief Visionary Officer

Twisted Networking

(401) 400-2428

www.twistednetworking.com

 If you choose to use emails to send follow-up messages, be sure that your signature line includes your picture, phone number, website link, and any additional useful information about you and your business.

TAKE ACTION

✓ Whenever you meet a new person, and you have a way to reach out to them, make it a habit to send a quick follow-up message.

✓ When you make your new connections on social media, send each a private message that says: "Thanks [insert the first name] for connecting with me."

✓ After your upcoming one-on-one, send an email using the sample template on the previous page. If you have their address and some blank cards, go the extra mile and send a handwritten note.

Chapter 8: Names

"Remember that a person's name is, to that person, the sweetest and most important sound in any language."
(Dale Carnegie)

How often have you said, or have you heard someone else say, "I'm so bad with names?" Whenever I hear this, I cringe because names are part of every culture, and they are the most significant connection to a person's identity, uniqueness, personality, and individuality. Like Dale Carnegie said, a person's name is the most important word in the world to them.

Growing up, I had a love hate relationship with my name. Primarily because teachers could not seem to pronounce it properly, and kids would crack jokes about it. People would butcher it. People would ask me, *what does it mean? How did your parents come up with that? Where are you really from?* As a child, I did not know how to respond. As an introvert, I did not want to respond. I would just shrug my shoulders, completely embarrassed, and dreaded the next time I was asked my name. I was always made to feel like my name was too complicated and "too ethnic." On many occasions, I wished that I had a simple traditional American name.

My birth name is Jevonya (pronounced Ja-Von-Ya) Jenkins. I remember asking my mother how she came up with my name. She told me that she was watching a game show and she thought she heard that one of the contestants' names sounded something like my name, but the name was Tonya. I was not too impressed by this story. I am not sure exactly what I was hoping to hear, but given that Jevonya is such a unique name, I felt that it should have had a more profound origin. I recently asked her again and along with the first story, she added that she liked the name Tonya and she wanted something that sounded like Jehovah, the creator of the universe. She creatively put Jehovah and Tonya together and came up with Jevonya. Now my curiosity was satisfied, and I was impressed.

As an adult, I still get the mispronunciations, but I kindly make the corrections. When I get the origin questions, I can now proudly respond by saying that I was named after the creator of the universe, Jehovah. But I still hesitate whenever I am asked, "What's the name on that order?"

Part of owning being an introvert is also fully accepting the name that I have been given. I like to say that I have finally grown into my name, but I still have challenges owning it. If you have a non-traditional name like I do, I am sure you understand my pain, especially if you are also an introvert.

As I have learned about names and how important they are, I value my name's distinctiveness. There aren't too many other Jevonya's out there in the world.

 When you come across a unique name, simply ask for the correct pronunciation and if you have a name that others have difficulties with, be patient and kindly share the proper pronunciation.

The people that we connect with are as attached to their names as we are to ours. Some might have a more complicated relationship with their name like me, while others might be in love with their name. Knowing the value of names and making a point to use them well will help you become a master networker.

How to use Names to become a
Master Networker

Many people struggle with remembering and pronouncing names correctly. I pride myself on making remembering and pronouncing names a priority. Everyone has a name, and when we use it correctly, we are better able to build rapport and make good lasting impressions. Forgetting names or calling people by the wrong names will have a negative impact on your personal and business relationships. When we try to pronounce a person's name correctly, we show them that we value them and that what's important to them is also important to us.

If you find remembering and pronouncing names to be challenging, here is how to improve:

1. First, refrain from saying, "I'm bad with names." This is the worst thing that you can say because

your brain will listen, and you will continue to be bad with names.

2. Create an affirmation such as "I'm getting better at remembering and pronouncing unique names correctly." (Refer back to Chapter 2 on affirmations.)

3. After an introduction with someone, repeat their name back to them. If it is a unique name, ask them to spell it for you. Remember the grade school refrain, "say it, spell it, say it."

4. Take a moment to write it down or type it into your phone.

5. Associate the name with someone that you know who has a similar name.

6. Repeat their name at least three times during your conversation.

7. If appropriate offer a sincere compliment about their name. (We will discuss compliments in the next chapter.)

8. Keep in mind that if you want people to remember you and your name, you need to make a conscious effort to remember them and their names.

TAKE ACTION

✓ The next time that you interact with a service provider, ask their name and thank them for their service using their name.

✓ If someone has a name tag when you go shopping or to a restaurant, use their name when conversing with them.

✓ Ask your new connections the names of their family members and use this information in your conversations.

✓ Use your new connections name in any follow-up correspondence.

✓ Find opportunities to use people's name and observe their reactions.

Chapter 9: Compliments

"Everybody likes a compliment."

(Abraham Lincoln)

Sadly, we live in a society where people seem to shine a spotlight on other people's deficiencies and mistakes. Frequently at home, in the workplace, on social media, and even in our own heads, we can only see what we and others are doing wrong and what we need to work on. Even if we do not realize it, most of us are craving kind words of encouragement and support.

I have always felt awkward when someone would give me a compliment. I would not know how to respond. I would deflect the compliment and spin it around to point out what I perceived as one of my flaws. I remember having someone tell me that I needed to learn how to take a compliment. Well, I immediately felt attacked, but that statement stuck with me, and it led me to research how to take a compliment. I learned a few fascinating things that I had never thought of. First, I learned through a study published in the Journal of Experimental Social Psychology that "people with low self-esteem have more trouble accepting compliments because they doubt the sincerity, coupling the usual feeling of embarrassment with a deeper underlying humiliation in which they feel that they are being patronized." (Friday and Journal of Experimental Social Psychology) Second, I learned that compliments could feel uncomfortable if the words you hear do not align with the way you view yourself. Affirmations come in handy to combat this. Third, I learned that compliments could make you feel embarrassed if you want to be humble; you might see compliments as a form of bragging, and nobody likes a braggart. These three insights resonated tremendously with me. They helped me to understand my struggle with receiving compliments.

Conversely, I learned that if you struggle with accepting compliments, you will most likely struggle with giving compliments. For introverts, many of us would prefer to say the least number of words possible. In our effort to avoid being the center of attention, we would love for people not to notice that we are there, never mind consciously choosing to use our words to attract people to us.

Despite all these challenges, since we love to connect with people, we can excel in this master networking skill. As Abraham Lincoln stated, "Everyone likes a compliment." A simple compliment can make someone's whole day brighter. Even if the recipient is uncomfortable, they will value your kind and thoughtful words. Just a few words of caution when using compliments to grow your network:

1. Please do not confuse giving a sincere compliment with brown-nosing. Brown-nosing involves trying too hard to please someone, especially someone in a position of authority. This is not what we are doing.

2. Do not give compliments in expectation of personal favors or special treatment.

3. In the business arena, compliments should not be used to flirt unless you and the recipient are able to be in a relationship.

4. Avoid giving compliments just to receive a compliment in return.

5. Do not overdo it. One or two compliments in a setting is enough.

How to use Compliments to become a

Master Networker

In order to authentically give and successfully receive compliments, you must have the right mindset. Here a few thoughts to keep in mind:

1) Genuine compliments are designed to build the other person up.

2) Compliments show respect, admiration, approval, gratitude, and appreciation.

3) When you compliment someone, it should be authentic and come from the right place with good motives.

4) Compliments should magnify the other person's strengths and good qualities, not their weaknesses.

5) Compliments should be specific.

TAKE ACTION

✓ Start by giving your family, friends, and close acquaintances compliments that you have not used before. For example, trying using a few of these morale-boosting compliments:

- You are a strong person.
- You truly inspire me.
- You are a great listener.
- The world is a better place because of you.
- You are so thoughtful.
- I love your creativity.
- Your smile is awesome.
- You have a great sense of style.
- I appreciate having you in my network.

✓ You might do well to begin complimenting yourself for your many accomplishments, big and small.

This action step ties in nicely with Chapter 2 on Affirmations. Affirmations can also be written as compliments to ourselves. The more you see yourself in a positive light and you become relatively comfortable hearing positive words about yourself, the more you will be able to compliment others for their good qualities. It is extra important to be generous toward yourself if you want to be generous toward others.

Chapter 10: The Power of a Smile

"Your smile will give you a positive countenance that will make people feel comfortable around you." (Les Brown)

As I write this tip, I cannot help but have a smile on my face. I love to smile, and I love to see other people smile. I believe that smiling is the most underrated relationship building tool in our toolbox. A smile has been coined as the "universal language." So much is communicated when you smile at another person. A smile demonstrates confidence, makes you more attractive to others, invigorates other people and can instantly change the mood in a room.

There are links between good health, longevity, and smiling. Some of these benefits include:

- relieving stress
- boosting the immune system
- lowering blood pressure and

- making you look younger

There was a time when I would hide my smile because when you smile, you are also seen as friendly, pleasant, successful, and positive. Where I come from, those were not traits that were encouraged. I did not feel good inside, and I also didn't feel comfortable sharing my emotions with other people but as I started to allow myself to be me and accept being an introvert, I also found the power in my smile.

Before passing away, one of my friends would always tell me that I had a beautiful smile. I did not believe him, but I mentally knew that he was not the sort of person to lie to me. With the help of personal development and affirmations, I have gradually overcome my self-limiting beliefs about my smile, and I have been able to embrace it. I use my smile to elevate my mood and the mood of others.

I use my smile to stay positive, to be more likable, and to have better relationships. I find that smiling makes me happier, more creative, and even more efficient because, for the most part, smiling always makes me feel good.

 "Smiling is not just a universal means of communicating, it's also a frequent one. More than 30% of us smile more than 20 times a day. In fact, those with the greatest superpowers are actually children who smile as many as 400 times per day!" (Savitz)

Many people struggle with smiling. This could be due to having a less than perfect smile. Perhaps you need some dental work, and you are self-conscious. Maybe you hold back from smiling because you do not feel good inside and you are engaging in negative self-talk. Maybe where you come from, like me, smiling has a negative connotation. Maybe this is the first time that you have read about all the positive benefits of smiling, or maybe you want to help someone else harness the power of their smile. Mastering this technique will not only draw people to you but it will also make you feel better about yourself. There is a direct correlation between the way we feel about ourselves and how successful we will be.

How to use your Smile to become a

Master Networker

People are naturally drawn to people who smile. Smiling is one of the easiest ways to build your network. When you smile, you automatically make a connection with everyone you meet. The more people you smile at, the larger your network will be. Understandably, smiling might be uncomfortable or might even feel fake but like the old saying goes, you might have to "fake it till you make it."

TAKE ACTION

✓ Practice smiling at yourself whenever you look in a mirror.

✓ Compliment others on their smile.

✓ Write an affirmation about your smile.

✓ Spend time with positive people, avoid negative people.

✓ Think about someone you love.

✓ Listen to uplifting music.

✓ Think about and be grateful for the good things in your life.

✓ Smile when you wake up.

✓ Watch funny shows.

✓ Sign up for funny text or email deliveries.

✓ Take out your cell phone and take some selfies. Take as many as you need until you produce one that looks good to you. If you are daring, post that selfie on your social media pages.

✓ If you need some dental work, do some research, make some phone calls and come up with a plan to have the work done. Even if you cannot have it done right away, establishing the goal and having a plan will make you feel good inside.

CONCLUSION

In the introduction to this book, I shared three stories that played pivotal roles in who I am today and how I have become a master networker. My experience in Head Start opened my eyes to feeling different and to becoming an easy target for mistreatment. At that time, I was too young to understand all the complexities of human behavior but today, I now know that my seemingly docile demeanor of being an introvert impacted the way people treated me and the way that I showed up in the world. Being an introvert is often viewed as a bad thing, but as the list at the beginning of this book makes clear, many of the world's most successful people are introverts just like you and me.

My first job at the South Side Boys and Girls Club taught me two important lessons. First, harnessing the power of your network can aid you in accomplishing big things. A strong support system is one that is ready and willing to assist you even when you want to do something a little crazy like jump into an eighteen-foot-deep pool from a twelve-foot diving board when you cannot swim. Second, just because I am an introvert does not mean that I am somehow inferior to others or that I do not have greatness within me. Jumping from that diving board was extremely scary but that experience taught me that with a great support system, I can accomplish anything that I put my mind to. It also demonstrates that introverts can be very daring.

My first business introduced me to the business networking scene. Networking has been instrumental in helping me develop and improve my skill set. It has helped me to stay on top of the latest trends in my industry, and has introduced me to mentors, business partners, clients and investors. Networking has opened so many doors for me to gain access to resources that have fostered my growth and development.

When I tell people that I am an introvert, their first reaction is of disbelief. I believe their reaction is justified simply because people still do not understand what it means to be an introvert. After many years of self-doubt, I now embrace my identity as an introvert. Understanding and appreciating being an introvert has truly been liberating, I can finally be me.

Although I still get uncomfortable, my palms sweat and my heart races in most social situations, I understand that if I am to achieve my goals, create the lifestyle that I desire and help others do the same, I must capitalize on my strengths as an introvert and continue to strategically build my network. I have trained myself to perform successfully in an extroverted world. And as Patrick Bet-David says in his book *Your Next Five moves: Master the Art of Business Strategy*, "Some of the most outgoing, magnetic and influential people I know are honest-to-goodness introverts."

I hope by now you realize that introverts are amazing people. There are millions of us in the world and we add value to those around us. True, we are not the loudest in the room, we are not always in the forefront and we do not like being the center of attention, yet in still, we have a way with people that is unmatched. We possess natural abilities that allow us to genuinely connect with others. Sociologists say that even the most introverted person will influence ten thousand people during their lifetime.

I also hope that by now you believe that you too can become a master networker. Recognizing that you can honor being an introvert while also stretching yourself outside of your comfort zone because the world needs you to touch more lives.

I personally still employ all these tips daily, and I know that as long as I am alive and in business, I will need to expand my network. Likewise, if you genuinely desire to become a master networker, you will also need to commit to:

1) engaging in some form of personal development every day
2) writing, reading and listening to your affirmations
3) creating and using your powerful marketing script
4) actively participating on social media
5) attending in-person and virtual networking event
6) scheduling one-on-ones
7) following-up with new and existing connections
8) getting better at pronouncing and remembering names

9) giving sincere compliments

10) and easiest of all, smile.

ACKNOWLEDGEMENTS

First and foremost, I must thank my God, Jehovah and his son, Jesus Christ for the greatest display of love. (John 17:3)

To my parents, Emanuel and Jackie Jenkins, thank you for giving me life and for always encouraging and supporting my goals and dreams.

To my sons, Carlos, Jorge and Christopher Allen, writing this instantly brought tears to my eyes. Adopting and raising you has been one of my greatest joys and accomplishments. I am so proud of the wonderful men you have become.

To my business coach, Ron Crosson, this book would not exist if you did not plant the seed and encourage me along the way. Thank you for believing in me.

ACKNOWLEDGEMENTS

To my Twisted Networking Facilitators and our many attendees, thank you for supporting my vision. Each one of you have played an important part in getting me to this point. I appreciate learning from you and working with you.

To my relatives, mentors, spiritual family, clients, and friends, thank you for adding so much value to my life.

To you, the fact that you are reading this book truly warms my heart. Thank you for taking time to read my stories, insights and tips. Without you there is no need for a book. I appreciate and love you.

<u>SUGGESTED READING LIST</u>

How to Win Friends and Influence People by Dale Carnegie

The Maxwell Daily Reader-365 Days of Insight to Develop the Leader Within You and Influence Those Around You by John C. Maxwell

Feel the Fear and Do It Anyway by Susan Jeffers, Ph.D.

Think and Grow Rich by Napoleon Hill

What Got You Here Won't Get You There by Marshall Goldsmith

Everyone Communicates Few Connect by John C. Maxwell

The Go-Giver by Bob Burg and John David Mann

Atomic Habits by James Clear

SUGGESTED READING LIST

As A Man Thinketh by James Allen

Doing the Impossible by Patrick Bet-David

Endless Referrals by Bob Burg

The Way You Do Anything Is The Way You Do Everything by Suzanne Evans

Rich Dad Poor Dad by Robert Kiyosaki

New World Translation of the Holy Scriptures by Watch Tower and Tract Society of Pennsylvania

<u>CITATIONS</u>

Augustine, Amanda. "The Importance of Networking (and How to Do It Well)." *TopResume*, 2020, https://www.topresume.com/career-advice/importance-of-networking-for-career-success. Accessed 18 February 2021.

Cherry, Kendra. "https://www.verywellmind.com/signs-you-are-an-introvert-2795427." *Very Well Mind*, 17 September 2020, https://www.verywellmind.com/signs-you-are-an-introvert-2795427. Accessed 12 October 2020.

Friday, Francesca, and Journal of Experimental Social Psychology. "Why Taking Compliments Is So Hard, and How to Finally Accept Them." *Observer*, 01 February

CITATIONS

2018, https://observer.com/2018/02/why-taking-compliments-is-so-hard-and-how-to-finally-accept-them. Accessed 4 January 2021.

Savitz, Eric. "The Untapped Power of Smiling." *Forbes*, 22 March 2011, https://www.forbes.com/sites/ericsavitz/2011/03/22/the-untapped-power-of-smiling/. Accessed 8 October 2020.

Statista. "Number of social network users worldwide from 2017 to 2025." *Statista*, H. Tankovska, 28 January 2021, https://www.statista.com/statistics/278414/number-of-worldwide-social-network-users/. Accessed 17 February 2021.

CITATIONS

The Myers-Briggs Company. "Introverts and Leadership - World Introvert Day." *Introverts and Leadership - World Introvert Day*, 2 January 2020, https://www.themyersbriggs.com/en-US/Connect-with-us/Blog/2020/January/World-Introvert-Day-2020. Accessed 8 February 2021.

US Department of Health & Human Services. "Office of Head Start." *What We Do*, Office of the Administration for Children & Families, 4 June 2019, https://www.acf.hhs.gov/ohs/about/what-we-do. Accessed 26 July 2020.

ABOUT THE AUTHOR

 Jevonya is a minister, a certified business consultant, and a networking coach. She is the Creator and Chief Visionary Officer of Twisted Networking, a business networking organization, that's mission is to facilitate welcoming, engaging, introvert-friendly networking events.

Jevonya holds a bachelor's degree in Psychology and a master's degree in Education. She has three adopted sons and currently resides in Robersonville, North Carolina (USA).